BLADESONG

Bladesong

The Martyrs of Compiègne

Ann Power

RESOURCE *Publications* • Eugene, Oregon

BLADESONG
The Martyrs of Compiègne

Resource Publications
An Imprint of Wipf and Stock Publishers
199 W. 8th Ave., Suite 3
Eugene, OR 97401

www.wipfandstock.com

PAPERBACK ISBN: 979-8-3852-3626-8
HARDCOVER ISBN: 979-8-3852-3627-5
EBOOK ISBN: 979-8-3852-3628-2
VERSION NUMBER 01/15/25

"The Candle," appeared in the *Carmelite Digest*, vol. 19, no. 2, Summer
2004.

Scriptural quotes are from
The New American Bible. Giant Print Ed. Nashville [Tenn.]: Catholic Bible
Press, c1987.

Flowers
for Our Lady of Mount Carmel

Contents

Acknowledgements

Gratitude wells up, and I am thankful for:

My wonderful parents and brother, John who loved me

Father Abraham Azar, Father Angelus Shaughnessy, OFM Cap, Father Ray Dunmyer, Father James Geoghegan, OCD, and all those in the Church who have cared for and guided me.

Carmel and the nuns at Compiègne, especially Sister Liliane, OCD, who encouraged me in publishing *Bladesong*.

Professor Tom Rabbitt, my excellent and exceptional thesis advisor, and Professor Robin Behn, a lovely poet and teacher, who both read a seeming endless number of poems about the Carmelites, instructed me in the art of writing, and gave me a beautiful new vocation.

THE VISION

"Fronds," she said.
She saw a castle of palms
with turrets of fronds
and fluttering shutters open
to the light within.

"Palms,"
she said.
She spoke of an ossuary
of lime,
a slow dissolve,
and of a secret ladder
scaling the sheer and wonder.

"Sheer,"
she said.
Banners,
streamers,
ribbons,
a secret ladder.

"Laddering,"
she said.
She saw in stillness
a predella;
steel, hushed and angled,
kneeling
before a choir of white.

"Stilled,"
she said.

Then a green redingote,
striped trousers
on the stairs.

"Chalice,"
she sighed.

THE CARMELITES OF COMPIÈGNE
MARTYRED: 17 JULY 1794

Then God said: "Let there be lights in the dome of the sky, to separate day from night. Let them mark the fixed times, the days and the years, and serve as luminaries . . ."

GEN 1:14-15

Lidoine — Reverend Mother Thérèse of St. Augustine, Prioress and Choir Sister, *aet.* 41

Brideau — Mother St. Louis, Sub-Prioress and Choir Sister, *aet.* 42

Piedcourt — Sister of Jesus Crucified, Choir Sister and Jubilarian, *aet.* 78

Thouret — Sister Charlotte of the Resurrection, Infirmarian, Choir Sister, and Jubilarian, *et.* 78

Brard — Sister Euphrasie of the Immaculate Conception, Choir Sister, *aet.* 58

de Croissy — Mother Henrietta of Jesus, Former Prioress, Novice Mistress, and Choir Sister, *aet.* 49

Hanisset — Sister Thérèse of the Heart of Mary, First Sister of the Turn and Choir Sister, *aet.* 52

Trezel — Sister Thérèse of St. Ignatius, Choir Sister, *aet.* 51

Crétien de Neuville — Sister Julia-Louisa of Jesus, Choir Sister, *aet.* 52

Pelras — Sister Marie-Henrietta of Divine Providence, Assistant Infirmarian and Choir Sister, *aet.* 34

Meunier — Sister Constance of St. Denis, Novice, *aet.* 29

Roussel — Sister Mary of the Holy Spirit, Lay or White-veiled Sister, *aet.* 51

Dufour — Sister St. Martha, Lay or White-veiled Sister, *aet.* 52

Vérolot — Sister St. Francis-Xavier, Lay or White-veiled Sister, *aet.* 30

Soiron — Sister Catherine, Extern, *aet.* 52

Soiron — Sister Teresa, Extern, *aet.* 46

Three members of the Carmel were not arrested and executed: Sister Stanislas, *aet.* 59; Sister Teresa of Jesus, *aet.* 46; and Sister Marie of the Incarnation (Madame Phillipe), *aet.* 32. Madame Phillipe would later collect the relics of the community and tell the story of the martyrs.

Bladesong

Looking from a window of her convent, Mother Thérèse of St. Augustine lighted an oil lamp and sighed.

Wrapped in a woolen shawl a peasant woman, holding a wooden bucket, stood selling her green walnuts outside the decorative iron gates of the Chateau of Compiègne. At her feet lay the strangled fruits of an ornamental chestnut which had lost limbs in the winds of the previous night. The towering branches of the tree growing inside the Chateau's grounds cast long shadows in the diminishing greys of the fall evening, 1788.

In their convent, their "Golden Fleece," in the village of Compiègne, seventy-five miles north of Paris, Mother St. Augustine's small group of Carmelite nuns followed the strict observance of their order in a life of prayer, mortification, and quiet. Cloistered, preoccupied with their rosary of days, they were little concerned with fishwives or kings; yet injustice and poverty did not go unnoticed.

SILENCE

Outside, rain like a slow burn;
this hearing more acute than sight,
hearing which conflates immersion
in water and fire.

Inside, the hesitant clock's ticking
as if in sympathy with our hearts
until in a narrowing of the senses,
we sense silence
strung across the evening like
a rich chord unplayed:

1

hidden rubric where we
begin conversation in blind sound
and blind wait,
surrendered, surrounded by amicable
encampment.

Though adjacent to the Chateau, a sometime retreat of Louis XVI
and his Austrian queen, the modest convent was far removed from
the worldliness of its neighbors. The convent received supplies,
correspondence, and local news through turnstile shelves.

The gatekeeper in this revolving world, Sister Thérèse of the Heart
of Mary, was designated "First Sister of the Turn."

TURNING

Turnstile,
revolving the motions of our lives,
bringing the outside in; reversing, the inside,
out.
Wheel revolving like circular notions returning.
Returning.

Turnstile,
orienting us again, yet again to the self
we leave and seek.
Mendicant to the world, we lose ourselves
in disorder's orchard;
gorged, we turn, like the well crank turning,
dipping our thirsty bucket, drawn and drawing.

Turnstile,
exchanging our lives,
until, entering into eternal Presence,
the spinning is complete,
a turning from and turning to; turning

until we are like sparks
spun from a wheel.

Mother St. Augustine was thirty-eight years of age when she be-
came Prioress. Despite her youthfulness, she possessed a grace and
perspicacity that would refocus, through the intense prism of her
holiness, the lives of her sisters in an extraordinary manifestation
of light.

&

I am conjunction
between the gilded *is*
and golden *if.*

I see into the soul's
cabochon;
I see beneath the filmy
moonmilk white,
the opalescent sparks
which start fire;
which whisper,
unspoken,
their unformed hopes,
their sidling doubts,
which groan for words,
for flame.

In January 1789, the abbé Sieyes published his controversial pam-
phlet, *What is the Third Estate?* In it, he urged the common man
to find representation within a National Assembly separate from
the Estates General dominated by the nobility and the clergy. In
Compiègne, on the River Oise, only Mother St. Augustine had a
premonition that dormant beneath the snows were forces which
would surprise the ensuing seasons.

WINTERSET

Winter's arctic leopard
had circled the world
leaving its frozen prints;

and now it leapt suddenly from trees,
whose black-brown limbs
shifted, unburdened with the icy weight.

She shivered in the thin-cold air.
Chrysalis wrappings in early December
hid the usual landmarks—
the wrought iron gate now
a giant crystal flake;
the small trees, acolytes
in lace vestments.
Everywhere surreal surprise.

On a similar day, holding
between her fingers
her mother's gold ring,
she had turned its circle,
wondering about the vows
which would govern her life—
its circumference—
tame sweet desire's sharp claws,
a circle, perpetual, sheltering,
through which
she would find her life
hidden, surprised.
She shivered
remembering the binding
which might, like Peter's,
lead to another.

The nuns of the Carmel, selected from the world and separated from it, saw the months pass into years. They remarked these years with their seasonal fare, with the flowering of their enclosed garden, and with the vibrant colors of the liturgical calendar—Advent, Lent, Pentecost—which they repeated through the *Book of Hours*.

ASYNDETON

Portico we pass through
matins laud prime tierce
Colonnade we wind the hours through
sext nones vespers compline
from the cool morning's moorings
to the stargate watch of evening

Steeple visible overhead
grey flagstones beneath our feet
smoothing passage
Sandals sundial psalter spandrel

Evening morning evening
asyndeton with elements
fastened on a curtain of seasons

fall (winter spring summer)
fall

Cycled circled cylindered
stripping gradually
the unessential
moving toward the gain of loss

In late April, the small new leaves of roses, green and lacy, appeared, and the orchards lighted the landscape with delicately shaded blossoms and the first tender foliage of the cider apple. Sister Euphrasie felt restless amid spring's impetuousness.

IF

Sidereal lasso which ropes the stars
and pulls,
plummet,
a wish to earth,
why is it we insist on *if*
as though the thought could, Proteus-
perfect,
affecting our fate,
materialize in an ordinary way?

And isn't wishing about worth?
What dreams we have, suffice
to add
a mullioned opening to the world,
as we, in novice calculation,
gain our lack, unnoticing
the vacancy exchanged,
absence displaced
as it spills into . . .

And what is it we lose?
Could Archimedes, in assessment,
express a clever correlative
of spirit?
Or would he even reckon
the magnet and impulse
which draw the world,
draw us;
each dawn—
need beginning over
and over?

The Estates General convened in May 1789 with several hundred deputies from the Third Estate, the estate of the people, elected. Meeting with opposition from the nobility and clergy, the Third Estate declared itself a National Assembly on June 17th and pledged a new Constitution for France and for the citizen. Less than a month later, citizens stormed the Bastille.

In August a decree of the new Assembly forbade religious to wear their habits in public, and on October 28th an act prohibited the pronouncing of vows in monasteries. In the Carmel of Compiègne, only Sister Constance, still a novice, was affected.

On July 14th 1790, the French people celebrated the first Fête de la Fédération. In early August, members of the Directory of the District of Compiègne inventoried the property of the Carmel. Armed sentinels were posted throughout the convent to protect the right of free speech. In the Great Hall, agents questioned the members of the Carmel individually. Each nun reaffirmed her vocation to a contemplative and cloistered life.

On September 8th, the feast day of the Blessed Virgin Mary, Sister Mary of the Holy Spirit, reflecting on the events of the year and especially those of the last few months, climbed the uneven stairs of the small bell tower in the rear of the convent's garden. She looked on a world in chaos, a world which had been as easily changed as the shifting landscape of the sableur.

BELL TOWER

Enigmatic airscape
growing beyond shapes recognizable,
into symbols stationed beyond
knowing.
In some different perspective—
aperch the falcon's wing—
would we see more,

begin to puzzle the picture from the
pieces?

Below forest follows fields
in inverted and gracious Greek,
or is it some other language lost
or yet to come,
signaling its *alpha* and *omega*
in emblematic fashion?

If we could transcribe this script,
this larger hand,
the *Y* the rivers make
joining to a sling,
what message catapulted toward us,
what unraveling would it yield?

Are the shadows across the
earth glissandos
in the rising and falling

of a stilled speech?
If everything means *other* than it does,
and *more*,
perhaps, could we understand,
there would be nothing left to say.

In the convent's chapel, Sister Thérèse of St. Ignatius, esteemed
by her sisters as their "hidden treasure," knelt before the Blessed
Sacrament. Cascading roses, bright in their dozens of blooms,
mantled the altar, yet Sister Thérèse's attention centered on the
Host, captive in an exquisite ostensorium.

CARAPACE

Sequestered soul
aflicker in this midnight world, votive,
who sees above,
eyes which draw her,
meteor,
into rarified air.

Absence she understands.
It has a meaning more than *loss*
and makes the separation
from having,
a gift which hollows longing,
tempering it;
makes the pain of never having,
tissued wrapping from desire,
a present to plunder the fairs
of heaven.

Tabernacled carapace,
gaze fixed beyond
what we can see,
she is unskilled at everything
except the move toward Love,
a move, swift, still;

the heart's latch gate
shutting softly, shutting,
as if someone were always leaving
or arriving:
leaving a promise in absence,
like the crescent moon hung
in the outlined shadow
of its fuller self; or

arriving like the suspirations
of ocean waves
to fill the castle of an empty shell
and resonate in absence,
Presence.

October deepened the colors of fall. After first prayers, Sister St.
Francis-Xavier, anxious to enjoy the last days of autumn, walked in
the convent garden. Here Sister said the Angelus before the Infant
Jesus, who seemed to be wriggling, arms outstretched, almost out
of the marble grasp of his mother.

While the queen, Marie-Antoinette, played milkmaid in the cot-
tage at Le Hameau, Sister St. Francis-Xavier, too, wondered about
exchanging lives.

MIST

Early mist
paints the world in grisaille.
Familiar
disappears into artless shapelessness.

In my close cocoon,
before the sun sizes the day
with blue and green dimensions,
October's leaves appear ragged
patches
in the slowly articulated, mollescent
morning.

At my feet, silvery puddles
small enough to delight a salamander
and close by, the single petal
of a wind-rifled rose
curled back against its stem.

The way the tree trunk bends
trailing its leaves into the
unknown . . .
and I have escaped the immediacy,
the envelope.
In the fields near Guilin,
bended over the river to fill buckets,
my trousers wet from wading into
the marshy side lands of the Li,
I am wondering who is stepping into
my life, its beads and Hours,
before reluctant autumn bees
begin their symphony
bending the flowers,
and what is it we share?

In March 1791 an elm tree, old and diseased, fell across the lane.
The storm which felled the tree left in the sky God's scriptural
promise, an archer's bow, arcing toward the south, toward Paris.
Sister Mary of the Holy Spirit watched as laborers cut away the
branches to make kindling and then hitched the trunk to the back
of a cart to haul it from the roadway.

REFRACTION REFLECTION DISPERSION

From here to there: transversal—
color in widths (violet and indigo,
blue, green, yellow, orange, and red)
climb steep banks of sky to disappear.

Not Spinoza's algebraic calculations,
nor Newton's components of refracted light,
but past spanning present into future,
I understood in reading the signature.

violet and indigo

The past, distanced by decision,
lingers in the memory as griffe
that catches attention
when I would not have it so.
I remember small hands plucking flowers
from a neighbor's careful garden;
the depths in my mother's eyes.

blue, green,

Fields, lake, and forest viewed
from my cell window
become a revolving calendar
excluding all but elemental:

prayers punctuated with the bell
for Hours.

yellow,

I saw the bowed arc shatter, scatter
prism's various light, shards cartographic,
which mapped directions for a new order;
and no one even noticed.

My hand, cut in holding the directive,
bled light.

orange,

Nearest is farther than breath.
In drawing near, I still am found
without.

and red

I purchased ochre from the reddleman
and drawing
managed only celestial hues
with my new color.

Despite the unease in the exterior world, days in the convent continued in usual fashion, their circumference drawn around a life of shared prayer. At Versailles, the king drew maps to scale with finely pointed pens, measuring distances with brass calipers; Sister St. Francis-Xavier, measuring distances with a missioner's heart, read through an Indian grammar, marking accents of the strange words she found there.

ALPHABET

This rogue alphabet tries my tongue with
words, with fractured gutturals and pauses;
tumbled syntax which begs sense!

If I should say one thing, will I mean another,
(confusing *hips* and *hovels*)
guilty of a *double-entendre* without the slightest
guilt?

Perhaps intention and meaning will be convulsed,
garbled like a ruffled blanket of
blackbirds enjoying an evening soiree?

Will I communicate loudly, defining,
by inappropriate equation, *heathen* with *deafness*,
or will there be a gradual leaning into sense
as the shadow from my words follows sound?
I must remember (though remembering seems
no longer a *must* with me),

the importance of preciseness is diminished
by the grammar in love's gentle catechism
in which the generosity of giving everything away
includes the gift of giver,
until even the sense of who you are
resides away from you, when you first live at home.

If only all could see how my bright alphabet,
translated, grows green parables which, tended, flower

into grace;
just as the calendar's pages are turned, and

turn into vivid seasons framed by leaves and grasses;
just as frail paper currency is changed,
and makes its change in golden coins.

I think I've given sense away talking with my
great baroque angel,
guardian with sienna wings, saffron-tipped,
urging me to mission to a needy world.

France itself was in desperate need of prayer. At eleven o'clock
on the evening of June 20, 1791, the king and queen, fleeing the
country, were halted at Varennes and returned under guard to Versailles. In his diary the king briefly recorded the journey, yet made
no mention of the encounter.

At Compiègne, Sister Julia-Louisa and Sister Marie of the Incarnation made preparations for a play of shadow puppets to be performed on the Feast of St. John the Baptist, June 24th.

SILHOUETTES

Stiff eclipses
dueling small latitudes of silence,
of light,
from didymous poles, black, white,
are scripted into syntax,
fill a tiny curtained set.

Opposites,
definition and ambiguity,
coexist easily
in this scrambling of
opportunity;

while we, as audience,
in thought's scant theatre,
reversing values,
fiddle with paper latches,
fumble with niello catches
which allow our wanting selves

admittance to . . .
within the confines . . .

but not yet wholly admitted,
except to that surface;
there, finding viscous certainty,
we move horizontally
to outline's black edges,
character and scene,
an austere text, displayed
against a parchment ground;
a mental alchemy required,
a vertical thrust turning into
welcome.

Although Mother St. Augustine desired the martyrs' palm, she believed that true sanctity lay in desiring the will of God. While martyrdom frequently seemed silhouetted in its intensity against the unacceptable compromise of civil obedience, she agonized over her direction of the community. Remembering that Teresa of Avila had also yearned for a martyr's death, Mother St. Augustine addressed prayers to the Spanish nun who had illuminated, by her example, the Carmelite order.

MARTYRDOM

Neither to seek nor to avoid,
but to steer a passage through
safe desire
until we find perfect placement
having stooped to enter so small a space
as surrender . . .
this is our wish.

In that enclosure in which forfeiture
is complete,
in the tiny cavern which is self,
amid the thinning greys dissolving into
darkness,
we are led not by aggrandizement
of immortal possession,
but by a poverty
which takes its fill in nothing, in
emptiness.

Finding that our lives are the least
offering,
we regard with proper horror our
timid response to that brave question
which permits suffering;

find in abasement
our tongues severed from
familiar language;
then the astonishment of voice.

During Easter Week in early April, 1792, Mother St. Augustine re-
discovered the story of a vision granted a lay sister of the Carmel of
Compiègne who, in 1683, saw a community, clad in white cloaks,
called to follow the Lamb.

To prepare her daughters for the sacrifice she believed they would
have to make, the Mother Prioress composed the words to a Vow
of Immolation. Yet she hesitated to approach the community.

In the last days of that same month, the guillotine—sometimes
called the *louisette*, sometimes the *physician*—was first used in
Paris. Word soon reached the provinces of the horrific nature of
this new contraption. Sister of Jesus Crucified, awakened suddenly
one evening, stood peering into the wordless night.

WIND

Night wind through the alders,
soughing, sighing,
muttering the shutters,
closing the hallway door,
flickering the lamp's flame which flickers the wall.

Oak fingers scribe an unknown language against
the pane,
write in an insistent wooden hand—shadowed
calligraphy,
invisible, yet strong, compelling:

Therefore . . .
We want to read *therefore*

as if "because" was precedence of consequence,
linear;
as if the action water makes,
will make
a cup when poured into a cup.
We seek illative meaning.
But if precedence is mad and
consequence is fatal—
a living game of quoits in which the pegs
are missing,
inference may be made although sense is lost;
innocence is cost.

Like a spilled cup, innocence costs,
spilled like clouds which harrow the moon's face
while harsh wind turns the world inside out.

By a decree passed in 1790, priests, who had refused to take an
oath of loyalty to the Civil Constitution, were suddenly no longer
merely *recalcitrant,* but were hunted as enemies of the State. To-
ward the end of April 1792, attacks on the clergy became intense.
Only in secret could they offer the sacraments and minister to
their followers.

Mother St. Augustine suggested to the community that, through
an Act of Immolation, they offer their lives for the restoration of
peace and unity. On May 30, the Feast of St. Joan of Arc, the sisters,
alarmed by growing animosity toward the Church of Rome, ac-
cepted the proposal for a fourth vow.

ACT OF IMMOLATION

Reserving nothing
but our vulnerability,
the ballast of our persons
tossed into the dark waves

of lost,
we feel our way down
invisible passages, quiet corridors
which breathe the Spirit.
Far from the accustomed
resonance
of *accompanied*,
the metaphorical compass
which is the usual way,
we follow the binding, the
vow,
which summons courage
for our permissive stealing
from the firestorms
of heaven.

Despite the furor in the outside world, life in the convent contin-
ued as it had. Four times a year, the sisters hired an elderly crafts-
man to help with repairs. On a summer afternoon, while the old
man mended a rainspout broken from its decorative harness, his
daughter wandered in the garden, interrupting Sister of Jesus Cru-
cified as she read a book of poetry.

CABBAGE

The way a cabbage leafs
leaves inside leaves
inside leaves

Unwilling.
I am feeble, content with rigor's simple routine—
prayers: matins through compline;
choir, where I sing off-key (but beautifully);
content with gathering blackberries and currants
which climb summer's quickset hedges;
walks through the sparse autumn detailed

in black branches,
mid-day meals: steaming lentil soup, great crusts
of fresh bread, leeks and creamy cheese.

The cabbage worm must dream
celadon dreams
must move through
this world
crossing boundaries, visible/invisible

Unwilling. I am unwilling.
Âme, village savant,
likens my sure appointment with Monsieur Sanson
to cutting a cabbage whose head is gathered
in the gardener's basket.

"Were you not grown for God? Are you
better than the cabbage?" she asks.

And now I flee what I once sought;
exchange security's sure lamp for illumination
from elusory lights.
A dedication to the Passion, yet
passionless. Wormed heart!

breathless crawl
through green furled perimeters
frail spy
finding within the veined vegetable heart
what return for such a quest?

Make my prayer, Lord, insistent like
the willing moth drumming evening's window.

My heart's worm
worries longing's ivory spheres,

ivory turnings within
turnings within turnings.

Sister Charlotte of the Resurrection, the convent's infirmarian mixed a draught made from nettles for Sister Mary of the Holy Spirit. Sister Charlotte sometimes fretted over her work, but always in silence.

THE INFIRMARIAN

Salves and poultices, spoons and treacle,
leeches and letting,
my world is gallipots: remedies
for fever, abscess, dog bite, dropsy;
for liver, lung, and heart.

Today I find myself the patient.
Symptoms: no feint or fever, Sister Infirmarian,
but genuine fear, ratcheted, moving toward sure
terror;
heart and spleen obstructed; disturbed sleep;
woolen mouth; fluttering pulse; dark and violent
humor.

Prescription: (borrowed from Monsieur du Port,
physician, as treatment for a melancholy spirit)
borage and tamarind: balm which soothes and enables
dreamless sleep;
fiery apple for its pungent fragrance;
violet, hart's tongue, senna and prunes with whey;
the black hellebore for tears.

This regimen to no avail.
Almost a wish for Mesmer's hypnotic cure,
an unguent for the mind to ease progression
toward a thought

as distant and immanent as death.

What heals the soul's contagion?
For if I flee from my affliction,
I shall be like the unfortunate camel
which swallows its own reservoir.
And if I do not—
an introduction, *Sainte* to *Saint*,
a display of our national metal.
In either case, a severing.

Would rather, satisfying the emphatic expectations
of *much* and *much*,
wrestle the remaining hours of my bent days
in a lazarette.
Instead: the Text underscored, with *more*
written large in red.

Prognosis: trepidation.
A simple referral:
physician to *physician* to *Physician*.
Humor for the humor, Lord.
To find the cure allopathic, after all,
healing incompletion with completion?
And you as egalitarian as any *sans-culotte*.

Mother St. Augustine, too, found everyday objects and events reflected her preoccupation with the times, though for her it was not fear they evoked but a growing conviction of the necessity for sacrificial remedy. As she meditated on the balm of peace which she and her daughters ardently desired, Sister St. Martha's preparation of a potpourri took on special significance.

FRAGRANCE

Gardener gathering the season's remainder,
she carefully cuts the stems away
leaving an inflorescence, blossoms and buds.

In a wooden bowl rubbed with cloves,
She mixes papery garments of rose, pansy,
and yarrow;
leaves of lemon verbena and the laurel's bay;
vanilla pod, chopped; allspice, sprinkled;
essence of rosemary from a small vial;
and powdered orris root
for preserving pungent perfumes.

With her bone-handled spoon,
she lifts the mixture, folding
fragile ingredients chosen for
variety, for color.

She will lock the concoction in a
crockery jar,
in which, rinsed in porous fragrance,
it will whisper its secrets to itself.
When finally, she opens the lid,
incense will rush the air, the petals,
a demarcation, a flowery cairn,
that posts its notice: past to present—
remaindered beauty, existence transformed.

On August 10, 1792, the Tuileries were invaded by revolutionary
forces. The king fled to the Assembly and was arrested. Revolt
and frenzy spread throughout the country; alarm grew. The king
dreamed of locks, not the puzzle of making them, as he had for-
merly, but of unlocking them with keys of bone.

Relatives, in their letters to the nuns, begged them to leave the convent and support the Civil Constitution by taking an oath of loyalty. Sister Constance heard first from her parents, then from her brother, and finally from her cousin, a former dragoon in the king's guards.

BETRAYAL

Tucked within the *who*,
in the dusk of the owl's voice,
in the halftones of years,
the question repeats.

It is the letter I have received
which has roused the question—
the calligraphic script, imperative,
its vaulted insistence
rising like an old quarrel,
though there was never anger.

The renegade text
defeats my expectations
in indigo enfilade

demanding an exit,
although I have not succeeded
in entrance.

In memory's soft-lit candle,
I recall the friend, the kinsman.
Opening and closing the semainier
holding spent seasons,
I am lent only the earlier gentleness;
am unprepared for misunderstanding,
for its semantics.

This afternoon unlike the cloister of other
noons:
Mother explaining insistence, a visitor.
You seated in the parlor,
your eyes reworking the Persian design
in the woven carpet,
tracing the millefiori pattern punctuating
a ground of tempest red.
Shadows nibble light: scalariform images
nervously climb the wall,
reclimb it as if looking for,
as if looking for . . .

I wish it were as simple as subtracting,
of having and then not.
No memory attached to what came *before*
or the loss of *after,*
like the glazier
who one moment could see *into* and *out of,*
who the next minute fell from scaffolding
and was immediately addled.
I stand behind the oaken grille,
waiting.

All of France waited. In Paris, after the king's arrest, there was un-
certainty and confusion. The authority of the Paris Commune had
begun to rival that of the Legislative Assembly. Stirred by Marat's
journalism, the Commune stormed the prisons. Word of the Sep-
tember Massacres made its way to Compiègne. Sister Julia-Louisa,
married and widowed, understood the signs better than many of
her sisters. She saw that their existence was about to face changes
more radical than the occasional disruption or threat.

BLANKET

Even now the fields
are a golden gash
as if a magician's ochre
accident
replaced summer's liquid
greens.

In this richness
my heart swells
like the cricket fires
of evening.

I hold happiness,
in autumn's blanket.
There is no face except
the sunlight
painting its yawning
warmth;
its brightness fastens on
well ropes of
my contentment.

And already the contours
change,
reshape themselves
in the wavering shadows
of leaves,
their slow movement, narcotic,
as if hinting, perhaps,

a hesitancy to part
with the vivid voice
of existence.

Despite her calm demeanor, Sister Euphrasie was filled with doubts. Passing near the kitchen, she stopped, terrified, on hearing the word, *le couperet*. Catherine Soiron and her sister, Thérèse, employees of the convent, who had returned from market, were preparing the evening meal. On the cutting board next to the cleaver lay a great mackerel with glassy, yellow eyes. Knobby turnips, bright carrots, and leafy greens lay strewn across the long table.

QUICKLIME

"… le couperet . . ."

It opens on a word,
accidental,
easier than with passkey
or picklock,
that reflection on our fate:

Jésus coeur,
no catacomb nor catafalque,
no feretory nor fenestella,
but a quicklime pit,
a caustic furnace,
in which our immolation
is complete?

What is this burial
but a common ditch,
a loathsome lavabo,
an anonymous sea
riced with torsos
in a porcelain paste
of ghastly ingredients?

And will we be lifted
and turned on ghoulish forks

until we burn as flameless flame
in this earthly cresset,
or will we sink
heavier finally
than breath
into a ceaseless,
canescent cementing,
our lives not even ribboned with
the poorest measuring worm
in a forced ascendancy
of our spent noon?

Twelve o'clock noon, September 12, 1792. Sister Marie of the Incarnation unfolded her napkin and gazed toward the afternoon light. A flash of red outside the window caused her to think of the *bonnet rouge* and of the king's incongruous wearing of it.

EXPULSION

Beyond the windows, the topaz day
fixes the season's intensity,
reflects heaven's blue certainty.
Close by the cloister's entrance,
an espalier
supports a tree trained in
strictness,
the boughs profuse with pears,
golden, pendulous.

In the refectory, *Exodus*,
(soft inflections energize the reading)
the promise, rich,
strung on faith's invisible wires;
the soup, watery, impoverished—
the seen and unseen
exchanged, one

in the hope of the other
like the poised seed
trading its moist tomb
for leaves, for light.

I have witnessed the affliction
of my people . . . and have heard
their cry . . . .

Her thoughts shift
to the bland meal.
A weevil she spoons to one side;
prays to Our Lady for
contentment,
a *Salve Regina*;
then begins another:

". . . and after this our . . ."
". . . and after this our exile …"

Therefore, I have come down
to rescue . . .

She sees the door open.

. . . and lead them out . . .
into . . . a land
flowing with milk and honey . . .

Ambushed abruptly,
the noon quiet is silenced
by pounding indictment;
the stillness riddled
with viperous words:
fanatics, conspirators,
delusionists.

Words like serpents,
coil, strike, recoil,
violate the air
with their weavings.

Through the entrance
she sees the fall world,
its tinder.

Within hours, the Committee for Revolutionary Surveillance
seized the belongings of the Carmelites. The nuns were ordered to
leave religious life and return, laicized, to the world. The convent
itself was to be confiscated.

Two days later, September 14, the Feast of the Exaltation of the
Holy Cross, the day on which Carmelites traditionally begin their
Lenten preparations, the sisters, no longer permitted to wear hab-
its or to live together, left their communal home.

In the early hours, before matins, Sister Thérèse of St. Ignatius
lighted a lamp, knelt on the floor beside her paillasse, and medi-
tated on an image in her prayer book of the crucified Christ by St.
John of the Cross. Transfixed in ecstasy, she shared the secret of the
Divine transposition.

FEAST OF THE EXALTATION OF THE CROSS

down/
slant

Hung
suspended

the Word
above the world

convicted of
locution
spoken beyond the syllable

Message
with swiveled tenses
spanning the stress
of time

Plenary anguish
that loses
nothing with the hours

speaking cruciform
the opportunity . . .
and again, the offer
in commensal charity

Beaten gold
evoking the imagined motion
sin's reflexive silver hammer
brambled silver
striking sorrow
Heart's crossbirth
bearing
the Christ within

After their expulsion, the nuns lived in Compiègne in four houses
near the Church of St. Antoine. As she passed the church for the
first time on her way to a new home, Sister Euphrasie's gaze was
drawn to the wide grey-green steeple. She almost missed seeing,
near the steps, a pile of rags left for the poor. She felt herself a
rag, a bandage of charity, for her suffering nation. Alone that eve-
ning, she reviewed the sacrifices and the indisputable coincidence
the day had brought. She could not know that other remarkable

coincidences were yet to come, some occurring beyond her lifetime.

COINCIDENCE

In imbrication,
the world's workings
like terra cotta tile

designed to purpose,
multiplied, overlap
one, one,
to become a roof.
Or overlapped as triangles,
placed,
one at angles to another,
become the star,
the seal of Solomon.

This September day,
chosen for our feast of passion,
begins the Lenten practice
for our service
and our soul: today,
the Exaltation of the Cross
united with our haltered
leaving;
our cross,
eviction from familiar.

Though they seem random,
accidental,
date and deed
express a correlation beyond
the moment,
provide a patterning for the whole,

a parallel, time with symbol.
This imposition—
fact on fact—
lighted by reflection
allows embrasure
from this instant to the past,
the future,
the opening in the present
widening
to what we only can begin to dream
in our bartizan of hours.

On September 19th, acting under the vow of obedience to their Carmelite superior in Paris, the Carmel reluctantly took the Liberty-Equality oath.

Uncloistered, the nuns could no longer evade the law and were forced to wear the clothes of the laity. Sister Julia-Louisa found that she had grown accustomed to her Carmelite habit. She refused the clothier's suggestion of a *Pierrot* dress fitted in the jester's style. Instead, she chose for herself a dress of ivory muslin patterned with a flowered print of deliberate brown along with bonnet, apron, and alpargatas of twisted hempen cord.

OBLIGATORY FASHION

My tricolors
were never those in fashion:
habit, the color of cocoa;
veil, black;
cloak, the cream of lamb's wool.
And now I am forbidden those,
though only a pigeon
could be offended
at my dun-colored rivalry.

The State prefers I wear citizen's
clothes.
Fashion demands the *Constitution Cut,*
addressing loyalty with banded colors:
bonnet rouge, tubular dress, white;
sash of nacarat; and bodice,
blue, in the jester's style
(a parrot by any other name would
speak as loudly).

This uniform, this orderly outfit,
in vogue from gloves to garters,
tells its national tale
with garnitures, feathers, raucous
ribbons,
or bouquet (daisies, cornflowers, poppies)
tucked significantly into a lawn fichu
in patriotic fealty.
Chipped stone from the Bastille
reappears in rocambole and rings—
somewhat somber to my thought.
Fans, too, flash their sentiments,
fanning defiant flames
with a bold chronicle reflecting
the times.
I choose for dress,
instead of *parti* this, or *parti* that,
a simple shift from ivory muslin
wrought with flowers, an Indian design,
in darkest chocolate;
a white blouse, modest;
and canvas shoes with hempen soles . . . sturdy,
hardly
the colorful pumps which bellow
revolution.

The first year of the French Republic officially began at midnight on the 22nd of September 1792. Sister Euphrasie fussed with the observance of the perpetual calendar, a calendar which no longer recognized saints or feast days, and its unorthodox, unholy method of naming the seasons. A warped hoop, Sister thought, refused to turn under its tame stick.

The community of Carmel, divided, but united by the Act of Immolation and firm in their commitment to the obligations of perpetual vows, wrestled with their offering of hours. During this time, the nuns were cared for by abbé de LaMarche who came occasionally and clandestinely to celebrate Eucharist, hear confessions, and give counsel.

For the first time the Carmel celebrated Christmas outside of the convent. And so, the old year passed beyond its palings into the new one.

On January 21, 1793 Louis XVI was executed. People lined the streets to watch the coach pass; others gathered in the Place de la Concorde to see him guillotined; still others went about regular chores: tinkers mended pots; gardeners brought vegetables to the burgeoning markets of Les Halles; actors played in their theatres on the elegant Champs-Élysées. Images of the blade haunted the popular imagination. So horribly attractive did the device become that toys were made in its infamous design. Jewelers who had once imitated nature now fashioned working miniatures of the guillotine.

In April in the garden of the house where she was staying, Mother St. Louis, seated in the front of a small statue of St. Fiacre, watched a butterfly and thought to gain a minute's respite from a world distressed by violence.

MOURNING CLOAK

In March, in its leafless world,
before the azure hepatica or
snowy bloodroot,
you float in the breeze, down,
alight on a mossy limb.

Wings brown,
deep to purple, banded with ivory,
disclosing, closing.
Mourning Cloak you are like the habit,
light and dark, I would wear.
Velvet flutter.
In this drab season,
lighted only by the first furled
leaves of ruddy maple
and golden willow, you flower
among the branched arms
which plead a spring renewed by
grace;
whisper your secret like the gentle,
waiting blade: in closing, disclosing.

In 1793 France was at war not only with itself but with other na-
tions as well. The Committee of Public Salvation was established
in April to invigorate the war effort. In the latter part of the month,
Robespierre was elected to the membership; by the fall, he would
dominate the Committee.

That summer, a Girondin sympathizer, inflamed with revolution-
ary zeal to protect the ideals of the Republic, murdered Marat in his
bath. Word of the assassination reached Compiègne by mail coach.
His murderess, Charlotte Corday, was executed five days later, July
17th, on the guillotine. Convicted of a violent act against the State,
she died dressed in the orange-red robes accorded murder. The

nuns, sympathetic to idealism were, nonetheless, appalled by the brutality of her act.

In late July, Thérèse Soiron, returning from market with her provisions, walked down to the banks of the Oise. There she gathered nettles for the Sister Infirmarian.

RAISON D' ÊTRE

Stickly shade of summer:
the plumed egret fishes murky waters
along the river's shore of reeded marshes,
the brackish pools alive with colonists
from a dozen tiny clans.
Egret, what is it you search for?

Is it for a shimmering minnow? The fat one
you saw the day before,

like the suggestion of an answer which wriggled
free,
gleaming for a moment in the sun's light,
a minnow, to tease the question into lengthening
shape?

Or is it an explanation, roiling opaque green waters
in turbulent furor, gulped with no satisfaction,
elusive explanation, which, received, disturbs
reason's clarity?

I need to understand yet fear in understanding.
Is there an answer between the seeking and the
senseless?
I say so and daily refashion reason.
I understand, I fear.

One afternoon in September, from a window of the small study of her new lodgings, Sister Julia-Louisa caught sight of a cat whose slate-dark fur blended with the dying season. The cat crouched patiently outside the burrow of small brown rabbit. Distracted from her writing, Sister laid down her pen and stood looking out at the somber garden.

PURCHASED

The fruit of the sumac, blood brown
in the season,
hangs its lamps, dim and exotic,
against red brilliance, fall
leaves.

The drabness of one
accentuates the other
as the lantern of a vow
illuminates a life

and sets it ablaze
in volition's perfection.

From this vantage, the taller trees
become a background study,
their inky fingers writing
a text on sky
in a script so broad as to be
inclusive, open,
beyond the ordinary symbol.

Under the sharp wind,
the trees bend to the task
with a single-mindedness.

And is the end of becoming,

like moving out through the fingertips
into awe
until we write heaven's language?
Is the final breath, then,
of being purchased like
a lyric from these branched pens,
a lyric purchased
with the discarded vestment of
golden leaves
kindled in the last fires of autumnal
light?

Mother Henrietta of Jesus, devoted to her ailing mother, wrote her frequently. On the Feast of the Presentation of the Blessed Virgin, having received a letter from her family, Mother Henrietta mused over her response.

In the garden, the reflecting pool, clotted with the leaves of fall, reflected back patches of sky outside her window. Mother Henrietta dipped the blade of her pen into the collared ink and wrote.

LETTER TO MAMA

Today I heard your voice
calling across a youthful afternoon,
an autumn afternoon in bright livery,
and felt the warmth of being called.

You must not worry over the affairs
of the moment.
My future is secure.
My direction always *yes*.
No hesitation. No need for decision.
Sometimes easier,
like crowding for pleasure;
sometimes not.

Always *yes.*

Names are never mentioned
though I recognize myself—disciple and journey—
descending from Jerusalem
through olive groves and vineyards,
following the path, I recognize blind
by presence only,
my heart burning within me.

Sometimes that presence is intense, like
a thought
when someone else is thinking it too,
a thought which lives apart.

Sometimes that presence is obscured,
a shadowed figure that seems familiar
in its strangeness.

In the long, curious afternoon, I pray
with the disciples,
Mane, Domine, quoniam advesperacit.

In November the Carmelites heard news of the noyades in Nantes, where victims, many of whom were priests, were drowned in barges, the trap doors of the vessels opening to the wintry waters of the Loire.

On June 8th, 1794, patriots celebrated the Festival of the Supreme Being. The Law of 22 Prairial two days later made it easier for the Revolutionary Tribunal to convict those brought to trial for offenses against the State. Before the fall of Robespierre on July 27th, fourteen hundred people would die. The victims fell, in the words of Fouquier-Tinville, like tiles from a roof.

Sister Euphrasie, ashamed for the idolatry of the nation and fearful of the events which brought news of more bloodshed and terror, opened her prayer book and was surprised to turn to a passage which Mother Henrietta had recently mentioned.

AMBER

Caught insect in the long day's amber
translucence,
held fast, frozen, in midsummer's warmth,
fixed in my uncertainty, I wait.
Grain of sand
trapped in the narrow hour
between the coming and going,
I am no longer citizen of this world
or yet of another.

And is this hesitation, then,
pivotal vantage
from which we see past and future,
as if fixed in equatorial accident,
the sun so immediately overhead
that there is no shadow—
not the lengthening past,

nor the unraveling future;
not death,
nor still a dream?
Realizing the present, its power,
will we understand, finally, the passage
disputed on the road to Emmaus,
begin to see
essential from unessential,
understand no ambiguity of tense
from our centrality in context,
see ourselves as word, writing the page?

In June 1794, the postmaster of Compiègne accused the Carmel-ites of treason. He discovered scapulars and a canticle to the Sacred Heart in their possession. They were also said to have concealed the "crown robes," the tiny regalia of the waxen Infant Jesus which Sister St. Louis dressed each liturgical season in the colors of the Church, then adorned with lilies and a crown of gold filigree.

Charged with conspiring against the Republic, the nuns were ar-rested at noon on June 22nd, preceding the eve of the Feast of St. John the Baptist. The postmaster, feeling unwell, spent the day at home with his wife.

THE POSTMASTER

To and *from*
were his usual concerns;
he was intermediary,
the text between, no matter.

This morning
finding in his drawing room
a book of verse,
a silver ribbon marking
the *Tale of Salome*,
he perused lines,
read in monotone, undertone:

Salome remembered being breathless,
her breast heaving with the violence
of veils, of dance,
when they brought the heavy plate,
heavier still
with the silence of wilderness.

The head, its gaunt features bronze-dark

from sun,
seemed only to be musing.

She reached with slender fingers
to touch the cheek,
to touch the intensity, the wholeness
felt the shudder

(though her maid saw nothing).
The lids lifting slowly,
the eyes, raised from meditation,
fixed on her,
as a thin bubble of blood
formed on the lips.

Everywhere in the withering years,
despite a bandage of veils,
she saw eyes,
replicated, tessellated, imbricated,
in the hangings above the bed,
in the wick floating in the slow oil
of the lamp,
in the crisscross shadows,
the cypress limbs on palace walls.

The fox in her dreams
hunted the eyes;
the eyes lured the fox,
lured her
and she could not follow.

The eyes did not close,
would never close,
their dark chamber,
her only room.

He felt his wife's presence
in the complicity of lemon
and lavender;
forgetting the book,
he turned,
his eyes following her firmness,
as she bent to retrieve the small
marker
she had playfully thrown
in his direction.

For a moment, in her movement
he saw veils and blushed

as she returned to him
the affection saved
for occasions,
more lately occasioned
by his fervor as ferret for
the Revolution.
He reached to caress her thigh,
hesitantly sliding his hand down
the silk of her robe;
waited for an objection,
though he heard none.

That evening,
the fires of safety spent,
their embers dying,
he dreamed ghostly forms,
silent hooded figures entering
through the doors of St. Antoine's
at midnight.
Pulled, magnet, he followed,
found waiting,
a chamber of eyes.

In June, Mother St. Augustine went to Paris, ordered there by Father Rigaud, Superior of the Carmelites in France, to visit her infirm mother. Despite her desire to see her dearest relative, she had hesitated to leave her daughters aware that the time of arrest was imminent. Sister Marie of the Incarnation was also in Paris on family business. As the two nuns walked along the rue St. Antoine, through which the tumbrels traveled on their way to the guillotine, a cart passed with the next victims. Although Sister Marie begged the Prioress not to look, Mother St. Augustine remained still, compassionately observing them for several minutes.

By June 21st, the Mother Prioress was back in Compiègne. Sister Marie, with her father's estate still unsettled, remained in Paris. The nuns and their employees were arrested the following day. For the next twenty days, the Carmel was incarcerated at the former convent of the Visitation where a community of English Benedictines, who had been living at Cambrai, were imprisoned as well. It was here that the community formally retracted the Liberty-Equality Oath.

On July 12th, the Carmelites received permission to wash their few clothes. Meanwhile, having no other dress, they wore their habits. As they were about to eat their noon meal, the Mayor of Compiègne arrived. Despite finding the nuns in their religious garments, he ordered them to be sent to the Revolutionary Tribunal for immediate trial. At three o'clock in the afternoon, the nuns departed from Compiègne accompanied by soldiers. Mid-morning the next day, Sunday, July 13th, weary and dusty, they arrived at the Conciergerie, a fourteenth-century castle, which served as a prison during the Revolution. Paris was preparing for the fourth annual Fête de la Fédération commemorating the storming of the Bastille.

The nuns entered the Conciergerie through the May Courtyard. Placed together, they were forced into their cell through one low door; they had to bow to gain access to the room. Arranged around the walls were benches; there were no windows. There were no straw pallets, no blankets, and there was only one lamp they were occasionally allowed to light.

Mother St. Augustine thought of her missing daughters, especially Sister Marie of the Incarnation. She remembered Sister's small quarrel with her assignment in choir and of the misericord elaborately carved on the underside of her seat, a walnut carving of a goose being fitted for a shoe. Sister Marie, she mused, had never been comfortable with the sandal. Mother St. Augustine noted again that there were only benches here. She found herself contemplating the meaning of *peace* as she had done many times in the past months.

PEACE / BEQUEST

Not in petition's recurring abstraction
lit by a thousand flickering candles,
nor in the detail of
a tiny, dove-grey feather
do we understand, *peace,*
its quiet ways.

Not in ordered prosperity,
nor in vocation whether shoe or sandal,
where one pursues, the other follows;
not in stillness and silence ... yet those
are the usual landscape,
nor in heavenly benediction signed
from crib or crypt; rather

peace finds life in detachment from
false values, their tendril wilderness,
lies in alignment with, participation in . . .

The words "false values" echoed in her mind; before she could finish her thought, she suddenly recalled *Petit Park*, the royal chateau, next to the convent at Compiègne and Sister Thérèse of St. Ignatius's description of a girlhood visit to the gardens.

ROWLOCK

Balustraded terraces surround their costly cage,
trail broad stairs descending from the chateau
to the formal garden's mezzanine to the lawn,
green seeking the horizon's expanse.
There paths converge, drawn toward the Oise.

Fleeing the boxwood hedges, the flowing guilloche:
flower beds in season's bloom—cornflower,
crocus, cabbage rose;

past cascades tumbling over marble steps into
great pools marbled with fish in brilliant golds;

past statuary, frozen from myth;
past pots with camellia and frangipani;
past trellises supporting clematis and honeysuckle;

past tubs of lime and lemon, we discover
forest walks—broad allées,
bounded by chestnut, beech, elm,
that wind through woods, intersect, approach
pavilions, temples, bridges—
temporary prayer-rooms, where we

like oars at rest in the rowlock,
await the rower.

Mother St. Augustine's reflections were interrupted by the screams of a terrified prisoner. Tomorrow, she thought, there would be answers. Once more she fell into prayerful reverie.

Sister Euphrasie was awakened at three o'clock in the morning by a dream. In it the soldiers arrived again at the convent door, knocking, and shouting oaths. She woke with her heart beating wildly, her sleeve soaked with perspiration from her forehead, which had rested on her arm. Outside the cell, she heard voices but she could not distinguish the words.

TOUT PASSANT

The whispers are walls.
Sibilant they edge anxiety;
or indistinct murmurings, they surround
like the easy fence work which runs circles,
lacking painterly perspective,
in an antique tapestry,
a tapestry alive
which keeps me, medieval creature,
captive
among the thousand feral flowers
bloomed in hell.
Voices vanish in midnight's taloned
grasp,
who, in dusty beetle's livery,
whisper disappearance,
echo residual certainty
from stones in grey and massive
walls,
from rounded towers.

Shut in this prison
with its cross-vaulted halls,
its stairs, turning closely upon

themselves,
circular, scribing
in narrow winding
a steep descent in desperation,
I am the whisper hanging
in the air
already made spirit by the
darkness.
Life, diminished now
to a small swatch, the courtyard sky
above the confines of the Women's Yard,
do you promise still
an azure sleep
beyond the bordered language
of walls?

Twice a day the nuns could exercise in the Women's Court, a small yard bounded by the prison walls. A basin of water allowed them clean hands and faces.

They refused the prison masses said by priests who had pledged their allegiance to the State. Instead, the sisters read psalms aloud. St. Teresa of Avila, the Mother Prioress reminded them, wrote that Jesus casts his beloved into prison to set them free. This was, she told them fondly, their *armoire de fer*.

On the way to the courtyard each morning and evening, the sisters passed through *la Salle de Gens d'Armes*, a large hall filled with prisoners and guards. There they saw prisoners practicing, with drama and grace, before an imaginary guillotine. Others were writing letters to loved ones. These letters, the prosecutor, Fouquier-Tinville, would divert.

Sometimes as the nuns passed through the narrow exit hall, they caught a glimpse of a prisoner in *la Salle de la Toilette* being prepared for the guillotine, hair being trimmed away from the neck so that the blade could cut crisply and quickly.

Each afternoon the prisoners awaited the "evening news" of the next day's victims. From her cousin, Mulot, imprisoned with them, Sister Euphrasie learned of Marie-Antoinette's lost slipper on the stairs to the guillotine and of the King's repugnance at having his hands tied at his execution. In careful detail Mulot told of Marie Grosholtz whose duty it was to follow the tumbrels and make models of the famous and infamous for the Paris Wax Museum of Phillipe Curtius.

LE CABINET DE CIRE

On what orders
does she follow the tumbrels
to their destination
and by uncertain light,
suffering a stinking pit
of decomposing flesh
and chemical,
sort heads from
torsos before they
become the quicklime
of their burial?

And shall I be a grisly
memento,
death's buzzard
wiping the blood and bran
from my severed head
across her apron's wide
pockets,
all the while
smoothing my features
with linseed, oiling them,

tending my toilet
as tenderly as love?

Will she, with fingers more dead
than mine,
mix a consistency of plaster,
fixing the mask
across my unbreathing face
from which the wax would make
a second?
And then,
with small scissors,
will she clip a length of hair
to match an unbecoming wig?

Effected so,
shall I be raised atop
a macabre pike in a museum
of horror—
speared, smeared,
grotesquely rendered—
that a public may
appreciate a terror
comprehended secondhand,
my death unnoticed?

In the Conciergerie, the Carmelites were befriended by a vine-
dresser, Monsieur Blot from Orléans, who grew the grape for Au-
vergnat Rouge. Because his was the duty of serving meals to the
prisoners, he was given free access and was able to bring news and
small supplies. He smuggled charcoal, small sticks of burnt wood,
and a scrap of paper on which Sister Julia-Louisa wrote the words
of a canticle for the occasion of the Feast of Our Lady of Mount
Carmel.

The next morning, July 17th, the morning set for the trial before the Revolutionary Tribunal, Sister Marie-Henrietta awoke still in the net of her dreams.

AUJOURD'HUI

"Get up! Get up!
Quicker. Quicker.
Please. Oh, please.
Aujourd'hui."

She was dreaming the bluebird,
its musical exhortation.
Window on her childhood—
the pear blooming the spring
outside her morning pillow.

With excitement, she struggled
from sleep,
eager to see the lamb snuggled in its
crib filled deep with straw.

She thought of tag with her brother,
of later gathering luscious cabbage weed
to chop for salad;
of mixing stew stirred to the consistency
of mud in great bowls;
adding pebbles for potatoes,
wild onion for seasoning;
of missioning to the neighbor's children;
distributing a plentiful meal
and later small, crinkled pamphlets
urging conversion for sinners,
of gathering first violets from the woods
nearby,
flowers to honor the Virgin;

of full force tilting into
the expectation of gypsy hours.
Today she woke, stranger to the hour,
the prison's hoarse darkness and stench
contrast to the borrowed bliss
of remembrance.

Amid her heart's protest,
she began her morning prayers,
setting out once more to gather
woodland violets.
Today there were no violets,
only full-blown roses grown rampant
across forest paths
and everywhere the velvet scent
of heaven.

In 1794, Year II of the Republic's new calendar, the twenty-ninth
of Messidor was a Thursday. Fifty-four accused persons were tried
that day; thirty-five in the Court of Justice, renamed the Court-
room of Liberty, among them the sixteen Carmelites and Mulot de
la Ménardière.

The public prosecutor, Antoine Quentin Fouquier-Tinville, seated
at a small polished desk in front of the Tribunal, viewed those on
trial with what for them was an uncomfortable intensity.

At the front of the courtroom, near the Revolutionary Tribunal, an
artist set up his easel.

LABARUM

He adjusts the easel slightly, thinking
to catch the arched light from lofty windows
which lend the court's broad, vaulted masonry
its ginger tones in streaming banners.

He sketches quickly the scene
within the larger scene.
There is no surprise in this
Tarpeian drama of the Revolution.

He has chosen his subjects for
ideology, their contrast.
He could have read the record
from the "Court of Blood"
and rendered the same picture;
perhaps have drawn it surer
from the text,
from somber imagination's colors:
the edges of canvas, the edges of injustice
the same as those yesterday,
the same as those tomorrow.
In that way it is a scene
which he knows, yet does not know.

Presently, he squints and measures
mysteriously for perspective
in this, The Hall of Liberty.
He notes the busts—Brutus, Marat, Le Pelletier;
the tablets of law;
the official republican dress, the cocked hats
with red plumes.
The prosecutor is easy to capture,
the women, elusive,
except for their Carmelite habits,
massing in creams and browns.
One has stepped forward and is addressing
the court, asking for explanation.
The crowd's attention focuses
on her intensity.
Beside her the Prioress clutches her crucifix,

her thumb constantly smoothing its surface.
Another, an extern, visibly pale,
is supported by her sisters.

He cannot paint what he sees—
the serenity, the expression;
what he hears—the courage, the resolution.
He recalls the iconographer
laying a consecrated Host on a panel
carved from fragrant wood,
praying over his work before beginning:
the earnest intention expressed in
halo, and leafed gold, the colors bright, taut,
and the depiction,
despite the stiff Byzantine figures,
of sanctity.

In its literalness, he is painting
the wrong picture.
In his mind he sees,
from the serpent's skin,
the dove's wing rising.

It was 10:20 in the morning. Sister Marie-Henrietta heard the words of the prosecutor in which he denounced the Carmelites as traitors and fanatics. Interjecting a question, the young nun asked the meaning of *fanatics*. Fouquier-Tinville angrily explained that their practice of religion had condemned both her and her sisters. Sister Marie-Henrietta, satisfied that they were not accused of *Incivism,* said nothing more. She watched as the prosecutor gestured, searching for a word he could not find. He was distracted regretting an eruption of temper with his wife over breakfast, an outburst caused by a shattered porcelain cup.

ECCE HOMO

In the gesture: accusation,
significance;
not exclusion or condemnation,
though both existed in it,
but discernment of that
which went beyond
pointing out the one or two,

a common guilt stirring,
inclusive, reflexive.

The prosecutor, infamous
for his coupling in the crimes
of ochlocratic rule,
his brow, sinuous,
his skeletal finger fixing attention,
(heads craning to see the miscreant)
addresses the court.
The shadow from his lifted hand
becomes, in the subtle light,
the same shadow as myself
so that the end of one, the beginning
of the other,
blur into a single condemnation.

For different reasons,
it is result of treason, nonetheless.
And I can feel antipathy and kin
at once.

The light in the courtroom altered. The presiding judge, Monsieur
Scellier, of Compiègne, shifted uncomfortably in his chair.

Sister Euphrasie noticed the shadow of the public prosecutor, Fouquier-Tinville, overlapped that of Sister Marie-Henrietta. Mother St. Louis frequently likened the young nun to the Jacqueminot she grew in her garden. Today Sister Marie-Henrietta was aglow with a fervent beauty in the fire of her belief.

SHADOW

Shadows from this restive day
mingle strangely:
one accused of outlawry
and another who is no friend to law.

What is this shadow shape,
insubstantial,
whose possibility we carry everywhere
yet seldom notice for its lightness?

Is it a lesser self, a portion thwarted,
that reaches only half its plan;

or is it, rather, the umbrage of a greater view
having become more than ever we expected?

Shadow world pinned to this one
in odd patterning,
in hues, grey and brown, aureoles
of gold,
what casement are you for our lives?

And I shall be soon a shadow . . .
The judge is saying . . .
"plea, plea" . . .
Shadow words from shadow worlds
barter for existence with our light
and are spent quickly in the leaning sun.

The sentence passed;
the past is sentence.
Neither a necklace nor a noyade—
no blunt response sufficient,
but a steel severing
for our crime
of shadow.

The Carmelites were condemned despite Mother St. Augustine's
request that only she be punished. Along with them twenty-four
others were found guilty; the Court directed they be executed. The
verdict read, Thérèse Soiron, the younger extern fainted. Citizen
Mulot, silenced in his attempt to speak, was sentenced to death
with the nuns.

There was the formality of paperwork. Monsieur Sanson arrived.
Since their hair beneath their bonnets had been kept trimmed to
penitential lengths, the Carmelites were not made to undergo the
last preparations.

It was after four o'clock in the afternoon when Mother St. Augus-
tine asked Mother St. Louis to barter her shawl for sustenance, for
the nuns had had no food that day.

THE SHAWL

Shell within shells,
in its present, its warmth,
her shawl enfolds her,
comforts her.

Scallops, scaffolding triangular,
open upward in a broadening pattern;
their clustered stitches are nacreous
in lustrous wool.

Her fingers, paler than the creamy
yarn,
stroke the fiber
as if it were alive.

She has a fondness for the gift
encircling memories of a loved one,
a fondness for the pilgrim's sign, the
shell, which signifies faith's victory,
earth's dust to be discarded
for the final future.
As she draws the wrap around her,
the shifting chills, age and ague
arguing hard even in the July noon,
she thinks of Martin halving
his goods for a beggar
and barters with a tricoteuse
for cups of chocolate
as sustenance for the fast
which precedes the necessary hour.

At a little past five o'clock the tumbrels left the Conciergerie. They
arrived at the guillotine shortly before seven, the summer sun still
visible.

THE TUMBRELS

It was a slow progress,
official, royal,
this journey past the last hours
from the Conciergerie's dusty courtyard
to the throne of the guillotine.

No recission of decision.
Arms pinioned, the condemned,
pushed into tumbrels filled with straw,

its dry sweetness masking yesterday's
urgencies, awaited their expectations.

Along uneven cobbled streets,
wooden wheels of ignominious carriage
stuttered the minutes.
Behind shutters and sojourn,
those apart from the madness
watched courage passing,
watched sore choice given meaning,
watched midsummer's flowers
solicit apology.

The guillotine was set up in the last days of the Revolution in the
Barrière du Trône at the outskirts of Paris near the Vincennes
Gates.

A cacophony sounded in the streets; wagons and carriages clat-
tered along cobblestones; street-venders cried their goods of fruits
and fish, scissors and services. And always, from all quarters of the
city, the church and convent bells were peeling, chiming, tolling
the hours.

Sister Euphrasie could not help thinking, dusty as they were in
their brown habits, that she and her sisters could nonetheless, be
considered fashionable sporting the city's stylish mud color, *boue
de Paris*. She wondered at the irrelevant thought. She thought, in-
stead, to chide her Lord for the obvious symbolism of dust.

Mother St. Augustine, sensing Sister Euphrasie's mood, whispered
a prayer. In the next instant, a young woman following the tum-
brels held out her hand; Sister Euphrasie, who had been clasping
her psalter as support, extended it, her words lost amid the dis-
cordant noises. Tracing and retracing the name in the front of the
worn prayerbook, the young woman would later enter the convent
herself, taking the name *Euphrasie*.

The tumbrels arrived. In Paris, the family of Charles-Henri Sanson practiced the bloody and violent skill of national justice. The business of executioner was honorable, if not coveted. Sanson, a large man, began each afternoon when his services were rendered by chewing hangman's root to enhance his capacity for violence.

THE EXECUTIONER

He maintained a singular silence
to the question
whether they could think
or blink.

About the other details
he was pleased to share,
demonstrating, in a cottage shed,
la mécanique with a man
of straw.

He never, dreaming,
dreamed the heads of those he
severed.
His was duty performed
with precision, with humanity,
a practiced art
which wore no mask but his own.
His was skill, as excellent
as the harpsichord maker's
(though he himself played cello),
which tuned him to the nation's cry
for justice.
His record—
twenty-one Girondins,
thirty-eight minutes—
expediency with a theatrical

touch
high on his platform
above the crowd.

And if he dreamed,
it was of his son, slipping
on the blood-slicked boards,
falling forward,
the head jarred forever
from the body.

He kept buckets filled
to rinse the worn wood.
The grooves of his engine
were waxed;
the blade, triangular, sharpened, weighted,
wielded the dropped edge,
three quarters of a second, the exactness
between
breath and death.

Victim, hands bound,
finally absolved,
was strapped onto the vertical bascule,
the plank lowered
like dough into an oven;
the head propped in a lunette,
the hair, the ears tugged forward;
the collar snapped, closed,
the halter fixed—
the rest, rhythmical,
cutting cleanly
just at the fourth vertebra,
if the victim did not,
struggling,
pull back,

the head falling
into a ready basket . . .

tulips . . .
he grew a tulip garden,
had a fondness for the lively look,
the deep, rich red
expressed in solemn rows which followed, one, another.
Every spring, new bulbs arrived in baskets,
heads which grew green bodies
unfolding into color.
He loved their suddenness.
Despite their solid look, fragility—
a scythe of wind,
the shudder of petals.

Sanson tested the blade once. The first victim was led up the six
narrow steps to the platform. On a side street, red carts waited
for the gathered remains. Late in the evening, so as not to attract
attention, armed guards escorted the carts to Picpus quarter and
the lime pit.

WITNESS

Evening hour, purfled
in rosy orange, violet,
frames the scaffold's shadow
as it stands brattice to the sky
assaulting heaven's turrets;
frames a history contained between
endpapers marbled in blood.

Faces, their surge and siege,
become an eye,
and I am pushed further than I
meant to travel,

pulled toward the center.

I want to be circumference,
impartial, aloof.
In the crowd's jar and jeer,
it is impossible.
An elbow, stir and sweat,
the flinders of the moment crushed
by movement.

It is the point between essential
contradictions
at which *they* have arrived;
which has found us:
both witness and victim, willing or
unwilling;
the event no longer isolated.
I am here, drawn into the picture.

It concerns me;
I reach
to touch the scar
which makes it real.

Abbé de Lamarche, dressed as a workman, watched from a small
distance. He caught the word, *permission,* still he could not hear
the conversation. He remembered Sister Constance and her fear of
the guillotine. The youngest of the nuns, she had been psychologi-
cally led to this moment. He considered the words which must be
transpiring.

Sister Constance, having no opportunity that day for her *Divine
Office*, had offered resistance.

PERMISSION

In this intractable hour
who would have thought
I would practice punctuality?

Permission, Mother,
for my prayers?
Permission (even the *r* and *s*'s
seek to squirm free,
find a path through the word).

In the day's distractions,
the alien hallways,
the uncompromising benches,
the attendant waiting,
the hinged expectation
which . . .

Never thought, never . . .
I neglected . . .
thoughts fled . . .
like the voices whose bodies
I sought to discover.
Even the windowed sun played
at decapitation
behind passing clouds.
Time, portioned upon the chopping block,
gave no contiguous . . .
And I delayed,
the minutes unconnected with the
happening,
hoping for . . .
Time yet for a civil act
before an uncivil one.
"Permission, Mother?"

Mother St. Augustine held in her palm a clay figure of the Virgin with the Infant Jesus. Sister Constance bent to venerate the tiny figure.

There was silence despite the gathered crowd. Constance mounted the slow steps.

THE CANDLE

Uprights support
the crossbar
making a temple
which holds the triangular blade.
Between the honed steel and lunette,
negative space,
like a candle placed upside down,
its flame defined as circle
by an inflexible collar,
the two halves, closed, empty.
Behind the scaffold,
the sky,
the evening illuminated, rose-dark
against the deepening blue.

For a moment she is distracted
as Constance begins
the *Omnes Gentes*, sung at the founding
of every new Carmel since Avila's saint.
As artist she considers spaces,
those filled, those unfilled.
Absence as Christian inversion,
she thinks,
is an extinguishing,
a beginning.

The planks sigh as if in anguish
with the weight they bear;
no other sound,
except for the mechanical slicing
of bone and flesh.
The platform seems higher,
the steps steeper
than those imagined,
as her daughters
in procession
light again and again
profession's holy candle,
until

Mother St. Augustine offered the holocaust of the Carmel a final
time. In ascending order of their ages, each nun first asked per-
mission from the Prioress to die, then assisted by Sister Marie-
Henrietta each mounted the steps to the scaffold.

Abbé de Lamarche, who had remained nearby, was suddenly
aware of the silence of the preceding few minutes as a peddler of
wooden windmills abruptly brushed against him and began crying
his wares.

THE SELLER OF WINDMILLS

Windmills! 6 *sous*!

bobbing hats crying *red*
crying *spilled*
as paddling the air
the blade goes down
as straddling the air
cuts down the wind
strange mill
steel and frozen

blade turning down
not round the
striped bowing wearing trousers
baking baking
no bread to eat

baking the blood like bread
and none to eat

6 *sous*! Windmills!
Little Windmills!

theatre of blade
no curtains to stage a death
doves cloaked and choiring
they do not die

jester? no jester
jester answers they do not die

draping stages
frenzied pale and wringing
heads in sizes
puppets puffy
pulled and parted
sleep asleep like peaches
in a basket
bowing trousers
sleeping peaches

6 sous!

while pebbles sing
they do not die
sing a dirge
pebbles sing

applause applause

Mills! Windmills!
6 *sous*!
Windmills!

The young peddler, stepping backwards, accidentally jostled a
sans-culotte who roughly shoved him away with his fists telling
him to be quiet and be gone.

Minutes later, in the diminishing crowd, the woman who had
reached out her hand to Mother St. Augustine for the tiny figure of
veneration stood, still pressing it to her heart.

PASSE-PARTOUT

Key unlocking the text of hearts,
not wrought metal nor cast brass
but simple clay:
Madonna held
to venerate;
the Ansate Cross,
a Child in swaddling,
held within the arms.

Key eluding the hours' mechanical
fastenings,
belonging to no chatelaine
with clasps and chains,
opening
as keeper and kept,
whose weight grapples with sleek
and glassy time
eking out the minutes,
one by one by one;
grappling with the hours

which draw us forward
through desire's mirages
through the slowing death
lived out in days
which, ineluctable,
drain away the pureness
from intention.

Key finding in any moment,
approach.

Abbé de Lamarche turned away from the guillotine and walked
to the river and then along le quai de la Mégisserie. He could see,
across the Seine, in the darkness, the outline of the Conciergerie
on its island, its lights flickering.

Meanwhile, workers, drinking and laughing, gathered the bodies
and heads of the victims onto carts to deliver them to the former
convent garden at Picpus. The limbs, not yet stiff, bounced in their
heap of bloody flesh as the carts moved along the way. Before ten
o'clock that evening the gates at the back of the garden were opened
to allow for the arrivals. The dead were stripped of their clothing
and thrown into a pit of quicklime. The stink of decomposing flesh
hung heavily in the air. Aromatic branches were burned to mask
the odor.

That same evening, Monsieur Jean Jacques Pelras, Sister Marie-
Henrietta's brother, returned home at a late hour. He reflected on
his sister.

CITIZENESS

No moon.
Carriage lantern fading into distance.
Darkness.
Yesterday the feast, Our Lady of Mount Carmel,

the cherry tree filled with fruit.
Persimmons lit Christmas their tree.
The white rose, dyed to crimson,
bloomed against the iron gate.
And now this glowing light which hops the stairs
then bounces back to await my step—
games: Hide-and-Seek, Blind-Man's-Bluff,
which you and I played as small children
in a safe, familiar arbor.

In the morning, they will bring me word,
Annette,
but that's not soon enough for you.

Last night I thought myself once more
the prince asleep in Echo's Chamber.
Remember how you played Florina to my Charming,
wailing the leaves awake?

Last night the trembling leaves echoed
the *Carmagnole*,
soldiered dreams along a cobbled street
were witness to the guillotine
which cut and corded my heart's kindling.
I heard the scaffold singing light.
Remember how you told me you would discover
the garden's secrets in the rose's bloom
as, petal by petal, you unfurled its tight bud?
How you told me in that same garden
the choice for Carmelite,
explaining yourself as *enclitic* for Christ
(you, the unaccented),
your readiness astonishing my heart?

Last night I heard the scaffold singing light
and today this light, binding peace

to my heart.
It's now, with that same readiness, Annie,
you bloom, petal by petal,
the red of the rose.

In his small room, Abbé de Lamarche sat reading again the Car-
melite initiative from the Old Testament by its unquiet light.

SOUVIENS-TOI

Elijah,
ragged in the caves of Carmel
above the sea's noon expanse,
understood the cost of prophecy,
the red words, urgent, speaking themselves,
a summons to fidelity,
a looking backwards for renewal.

Fleeing Jezebel,
the escarpment of her wrath,
fleeing the kohl-lined eyes, lids painted
magenta,
which painted his limestone walls
curious hues of violet rose,
he came to rest in Sinai's silent desert,
the color of terror transmuted
in mountains tinted shades of dusky pink
and orange,
like the flesh of ripe melons, exotic citrus
remembered from the lush valleys
in Palestine.
And there, on the ascent to Mount Hebron,
the sky lavender,
listening, he heard the voice of God,
a saffron whispering in the austere stillness.

And Jezebel,
pushed from her tower,
falling feast to the dogs,
did she, in that instant
before the jugular snapped,
with eyes widened,
see the prophet's wizened face
and understand finally the wheel
which returns upon itself
hatred, hatred,
and love, love?

Again, the message,
a testament in blood.
And again, a summons.

Hapax, apex,
the Word luminous,
the stars startled, rivaled
in their long light travelling
the years,
startled by the torch of Heart,
blazoned, emblazoned
in an hour of reflection, refection,
the scaffold—
altaring,
altering the hour.

Afterword

Sister Marie of the Incarnation, who had been in Paris when her sisters were arrested in Compiègne, was increasingly fearful for her life. At the moment of their execution, she was attempting escape from France in a carriage at the Swiss border. Not allowed to cross, she was turned back. A few days later at an inn in Besançon, she learned the fate of the Carmel.

ASSEMBLAGE

In evening's umber recesses,
in the sienna slant of last light,
the sun fallen past day's expectation,
the bruised world arranged in assemblage,
she wonders at this construction,
not quite an illusion.

She folds the linen napkin in her lap,
arranges it as she would fold an unwelcome
memory
which she will post into the future.
But now, for a while, in the deckled border
between shadow and night,
in the olive darkness,
she is as relaxed as the net the fisherman
lowers into the water.
Only later will she measure the powder
which measures sleep,
in a portion of forgetfulness against
the tensile strength of her own mind.

Disoriented, she enjoys this hour,
magically deceived in dusk's gauze sleeve.

Wandering smaller in the closing space,
she questions happenstance,
the net tightening around her heart.
Straining into the darkness,
she recalls Jacob sleeping on a stone,
finding the stairs to heaven.

Less direct were the stairs which Sister Marie found. Hers was a
lifetime of seeking.

THE NAMING

I marvel the name across the stone
with my fingers.
Chiseled with the letters
spelling my own name,

it names the entrance, the exit.
And though I recognize in part,
I am bewildered.

The door answers to my knock,
lifting back across the grass
exposing moist earth
webbed with roots and leaves,
unlikely lace,
exposing a silvery silo.

Stairs, in close descent,
wind downward in their casing,
like dark brocade drowning in a distant well,
like the beginning of indefinite decision
which first understood, later becomes opaque;
like the eye first clear
which Blindness sews closed
with milky threads spun from her marble

and constricted heart.

And what expectation here?
Some frivolous alter ego,
a mad mannequin?
Like doubt which redoubles upon itself,
I have reached an ending
or is it a beginning?

Although the Reign of Terror officially ended with the fall of Robe-
spierre on July 27th, ten days after the Carmelites sacrificed their
lives, Sister Marie continued for several months to feel uneasy for
her safety. When finally, she felt secure, as Madame Philippe, she
began to collect the relics of the martyred Carmelite community;
among the reminders was an alpargata. She now wrote down, from
remembrances of those who knew him in Compiègne, a sketch of
Monsieur Scellier, the presiding judge.

IN COMPLETENESS

There is a room he's never entered,
like the parlor never used;
or is it rather
the parlor which is used,
without the comfort
of the house?
Like a lepidopterist, he disassociates
realities, seen and unseen, admiring
only the still patterning
in a life he ignores.
Ambiguity is a space he cannot penetrate

finding its roominess
uncomfortable accommodation
with his constricted vision.

In Diderot,
he understands every word,
nothing more.
His bulging eye fixes an object
in a precise lens,
yet knows nothing of what it sees,
demanding, in visceral intolerance,
a fuchsia exactness.

Reasoning incidentally
he fails to find (like a blind man
having no concept for *mirror*)
that worlds exist within worlds,
behind worlds,
that the center lies *in*
rather than *across.*
In his cosmogony, there is no
substitution,
each being merely *other* in
separateness,
and nothing equals *greater than,*
except that numbers add.

And though he cannot comprehend,
his passion is for symbols,
work of Oriental scribes:
feathered brush strokes,
ink's charcoal texture,
and characters with dots like eyes,
whose hutlike shapes fascinate,
hiding with no subterfuge
the gathering lotus, seven cranes,
a lover's sigh.
In scrolls whose ivory-handles
unspool their treasure,
he studies the forms the letters make;

the flourishes.
He is a connoisseur of figures;
They slip through his hours,
calligraphic, cascading
dominoes.

In the spring of 1795, her research led her to Monsieur Blot, the
vinedresser, who shared his remembrances of the nuns in the
Conciergerie.

CELLARING

I knew them.
Individually knew only one
or two—
Sister Constance,
Sister Euphrasie,
Mother St. Augustine.
They blended, "the holy ladies,"
like the grapes in a ripened cluster
until their personality was the whole
against the bright green leaves
and vine.

I am not making sense.
It was as if, from their trellis
in the sun,
they had been harvested
at their most perfect
into a vintage,
aromatic; then,
cellared in a cool, dark
prison
to be selected, poured
into the most brilliant crystal
cut from light,

a luminous goblet at the feast of Christ;
their yielding,
the wine-red blood of Christ;
our savoring,
the blood-red wine
offered at the altar.

In May of 1795, Madame Philippe learned of the prosecutor Fouquier-Tinville's death. Overwrought, he had to be assisted up the stairs to the guillotine. With him, Monsieur Scellier, the presiding judge at the trial of the Carmelites, was also executed.

In 1823, nearly thirty years after the death of her sisters, Madame Philippe moved to an apartment in the Carmelite convent at Sens where she lived until her death. Occasionally she unfolded her woolen habit which she kept wrapped in thin muslin on a shelf in her armoire. She would muse for hours only to refold the garment when the light from the clerestory windows grew dim.

Remembrance of Mother St. Augustine's favorite homily haunted her.

OF

Preposition of possession,
illustrating a missal's page
with a double tail which curls
conquest beyond its winged body:
one a serpent's length of scale,
articulated strangulation's
gold-red brilliance;
the other, a flowering vine,
green-gemmed, allowing;
tiny rubric which waltzes
sidestep,
down all the side streets

which lead everywhere *away*
yet always nowhere more certainly
than *toward*;
small unreasoning argument which
argues for dependency
so that everything finally belongs
or doesn't,
possessed or dispossessed.
And is possessing what we think ourselves,
as owning's center,
the goitered *of*
of goosey pride disguised?
Or can possessing rather be a chain
which lets us pass through and through
gold links,
like back and forth through subtle
doors
hinged on ethereal proposition,
as we manage ideas, material owning
without the pickets defining
an absolute property?

What belonged to Marie now more than any material possession
was the story of her sisters. In 1832 at the insistence of Abbé Vil-
lecourt she recorded the history of the martyrs. In writing, Ma-
dame Philippe continually reviewed the past. Seated at her desk
she looked at Sister St. Martha's rosary; the watercolor drawn by
Mother St. Augustine and offered to Mother Henrietta of Jesus for
her feast day; a scapular sent to Sister St. Francis-Xavier from a
friend in the missions; and the head of a small statue belonging to
Sister Julia-Louisa, damaged as a result of the expulsion from the
convent.

LIBRARIAN

Always the wind's repetition
repeats its success with barriers, borders,
with distances,
insinuating itself as breath
into the shut heart;
there was no crossing then . . .
a geographic border
and no crossing . . .

Sorting and resorting thought's
transparent vellum,
I catalog restive memory,
relics of rosary, integrity
against the time
when there will be no one
to remember the story.

Posthumously, eloquently,
you must say silently
the urgency
in your existence recorded
here.

Rosary

brown beads, seeds, strung
suspended from a cross
carrying a circular prayer,
begun and begun;
seeds, like brown ants streaming
across a window frame,
carrying their tiny crumbs
undaunted by the task
of heaping up

Watercolor: Heart Pierced with Arrows

symbol of expanded heart:
a feast day present
gift from dove to dove;
arrows named with
joy and sorrow
pierce frailty,
pierce the dove;
brooding wings hovering
protect an unhatched brood
caught in their pale shells

Scapular

linen shield:
Heart of Jesus
and his Mother
which betrayed lives
but not Life.
Warrior and Lover,
lover and mother,
perpetually arrest us

Decapitated Head of Virgin and Child

mortal blow
arriving at the future
before us;
in the preface of things,
tell our story
of things to come

Marie died in January 1836. Cardinal Villecourt regretted later he
had not asked her to write more about her own life. He knew only

a few details about the hardships she had endured, being forced at one point, before finding refuge at Sens, to survive by eating the grass of the fields.

Among the poems in her possession, he found the following one. Perhaps she wrote it; perhaps not. It helped him to realize the uniqueness of Marie's own journey evolving as it did from the powerful testament of her sisters to their faith.

ALPHA

Haven't you learned that beginnings
and endings are arbitrary?
Were you expecting the mythic formula
which begins with *once*
and ends with *after*?

Everything has yet to happen.
It begins with circumstance
and moves to discovery,
or is it the other way around?
Isn't there an opposite way
to measure the ocean's tides?
The facts, of course, are already
accomplished,
as they were on that July day
when the clouds assembled
to witness.
The story is continuous,
it succeeds itself.
The expectation
is . . .

Endnote

In 1895 the Prioress of the Benedictine Convent, Stanbrook Abbey, Worchester, England (formerly the Benedictines of Cambrai) sent back to the re-established Carmel of Compiègne relics which they had in their possession from the martyred Carmelites. These remainders included the civil garb left soaking when the Carmelites were abruptly sent to Paris for trial. The dresses supplied the Benedictines, who in prison wore their religious habits, exactly the number of garments they would need for their return voyage to England in May, 1795.

A tribunal was first set up to investigate the cause of the martyrs of Compiègne in 1897. In 1902 the nuns were declared *venerable*; and in 1906 they were beatified. The deliberations at each stage took place at Stanbrook Abbey. The final stage of canonization has yet to happen. The Carmel of Compiègne, re-established in 1867, is today nine kilometers outside of Compiègne at a new convent in Jonquières. A small museum contains the relics and history of the Carmel gathered by Madame Philippe, while an adjoining room is a recreated prison cell housing the small statue of the Virgin and Child venerated by Mother St. Augustine and her daughters before their deaths on the guillotine as holocaust for peace.

The story of the martyrs of Compiègne is remarkable for the number of coincidences which occur throughout the nun's spiritual journey. The coincidences are revelatory of the significance of their offering, for example, the diametrical contrast of the martyrs' sacrifice of life with that of Charlotte Corday is remarkable; the lesson of nonviolence as an acceptable holocaust is inescapable. Coincidences continue into contemporary times, and, though disassociated from the context of the French Revolution, these events silently implore, through their synchronicity, the heroic guidance and prayers of the Carmel of Compiègne.

PROCESSION

Cusped arches,
their tight spades
opening to windowless capes
encircle the arcade,
enclose the cloister's garden.
Grouped in threes
they follow in procession;
and in the sun's light
light figures from the shadows,
insisting between the Hours
as if nothing is enough
as if even the sun
and sometimes the moon
obey an urgency
to prayer.

www.ingramcontent.com/pod-product-compliance
Lightning Source LLC
Chambersburg PA
CBHW060401050426
42449CB00009B/1849